# EXPRESSIONS

## Tameika Rahming

Nandra Publishing, LLC
Printed in the United States

NANDRA PUBLISHING, LLC

www.nandrapublishing.com

Editing | Formatting | Publishing | Designs

**EXPRESSIONS**

Copyright © 2019 by Tameika Rahming

All rights reserved. No part of this publication may be reproduced, distributed, or transmitted in any form or by any means, including photocopying, recording, or other electronic or mechanical methods, without the prior written permission of the publisher, except in the case of brief quotations embodied in critical reviews and certain other noncommercial uses permitted by copyright law.

ISBN-13: 978-1-950697-01-4 (Ebook)
ISBN-13: 978-1-950697-00-7 (Paperback)
ISBN-13: 978-1-950697-02-1 (Hardcover)

# Other Works by Nandra Publishing, LLC

Love Me Blind *(coming soon)*

The Artison Way *(coming soon)*

This book is dedicated to YOU! To all my survivors of pain. "You were given this life because you are strong enough to live it."

I would like to thank God Almighty, the source of my inspiration, the driving focus of my inner peace, and the reason for surviving. My little sister Nandra Hoffman, for believing in my gift, for the countless hours turning my dream into reality and giving my words a voice.

To my husband Bernard Rahming, thank you for standing alongside me every step of the way. I truly believe you are an angel sent from God. You have never given up on me. You have wiped every tear and crafted me to be the woman of Christ I am today. I love you! My mother, for your endless support and encouragement to never give up on my dreams. Lastly, to all my family—my big sis and to my babies (my nephews) Tyriq, Tabari, Terell and Elijah—I did this for you!

# Contents

| | |
|---|---|
| Acknowledgments | 7 |
| How Can This Be? | 9 |
| Stolen Innocence | 13 |
| A Life You Choose | 17 |
| Pain Inside | 19 |
| Waiting for You! | 21 |
| Incomplete | 23 |
| Do I Leave or Do I Stay? | 25 |
| Eyes TWO See | 27 |
| Losing My Identity | 31 |
| Who I Am | 35 |
| Finally See | 41 |
| If I Could Just | 45 |
| The Seed | 47 |
| Set Me Free | 51 |
| The Passion to Create | 55 |
| Beauty in the Face of a Battle | 57 |
| About The Author | 61 |

# Acknowledgments

At some point in our lives, we share a common pain during our path and for someone out there, please know that I share this pain with you. If my words can help someone find peace or if my words can be a channel to bring them understanding, forgiveness and strength, then I know I have fulfilled my purpose.

# How Can This Be?

I cried for many days
I didn't have any words to say
I woke up one day and heard what I thought was a lie
when the doctor said cancer, I thought I was going to die

Chemo and radiation was the only way
to kill the disease so it can go away

I lost my hair, I couldn't even bare
the sound of the razor, cutting so near
the image in the mirror I no longer knew
I vomited so much, my face was blue

How could this be happening to me?
Diagnosed with cancer at age 23?
a life I thought I would never see
scared out of my mind, all I could do is cry

I felt like my life was slipping by
I prayed to the Lord, my soul to keep

going through this was much too deep

Tears ran down my face
to a life that almost got erased
God, I beg you, please let me stay!
Let me see my family one more day!

I can't believe this happened to me
but in the end, God set me free
free from cancer, free to live
to you my life, Lord, I truly give

You chose me for this special task
I trusted you, so I didn't bother ask

A second chance you gave me to me
to help the world finally see
that the love you give
you give unconditionally.

# Stolen Innocence

My heart is beating, my stomach is weak
my hands are shaking as tears roll down my cheek

My mind is racing, I am steady pacing
I rushed right over and ended up at Clover's
I walked to your door with fear in my heart
I knew it was bad news, I knew it from the start

I fell to my knees and beg God, please!
to see your innocent face
the thoughts I wish I could erase
you looked into my eyes and I started to cry
the rage in my heart, I wanted someone to die

I know that's not the right thing to say
but my heart is broken, and the pain won't go away
I held you in my arms so tight
and told you, "*Baby, everything is going to be alright.*"

I took your precious little hands

and declared at that moment that I will stand

Stand for you and stand for the truth
though these are trying times
I want justice for this disgusting crime

He gave his trust and you took it that night
he forced you to do things you knew wasn't right
to hear the details of your pain
my heart broke in two
I nearly went insane

You came home with me that night
I anointed your body, I anointed you with God's light
and never let you out of my sight

Your innocence he stole but my
God will make you whole.

# A Life You Choose

Words can't even explain
the heart that is filled with so much pain
the damage that you have done
feels like a shot from a smoking gun
you pointed it at my soul
destroying my image was your ultimate goal

You killed the innocence of our bond
with lies of one who mastered the arts of a con
you played us all like fools with the
acts of a person so cruel

I looked in the eyes of a stranger
your presence made me shiver with danger
my life's truth I always told
your hugs you gave from a heart so cold
the love in my heart beats slow
whatever you reaped it's what you sewed

Remember that the hearts you bruised,
is from the life you choose.

# Pain Inside

## Pain Inside

Jesus, I surrender this pain to you
from the tears from my eyes
to the heavy sighs, to the time that flies
I let go of what was and what used to be
I find a way to finally see
the light wonders, the dark thunders
to silence the cries
from feeling that something dies
to the numbness inside
from the pain I hide, to the sweet goodbyes
this is my last cry.

# Waiting for You!

A pain that struck my heart in two
the desire of one day meeting you
every night I pray to see
what life could be if you came to me
to hold you in my arms every night
and tell you everything is alright
I long to touch your little hair
to wake up each day and see you there
to hear your little cry for me
to tell you mommy is here, and I will never leave
I wait each hour of the day
to get the chance to finally say
I am pregnant, and my baby boy is on the way.

**Incomplete**

## Incomplete

Every night I pray for the day I can finally see your face
visions of holding you in my arms is
a thought I could never erase
staring in your beautiful eyes until you fall fast asleep
giving you sweet kisses as I lay it upon your cheek

The emptiness in my heart makes me weak
in my dreams your face I still seek
the yearning for you kept me so drained
thinking of you is the hope I regain

The keys to my heart you shall keep
'til the day in my womb I feel you leap
not a day goes by that I don't think of you
praying for the day, hoping the time is soon

My heart will never truly be the same
from the day that you never came
and mommy is the title I never gained.

# Do I Leave or Do I Stay?

## Do I Leave or Do I Stay?

Feeling overwhelmed and stressed
all I can do is think positive and do my best
torn to stay or torn to leave
to find a new direction out of these
to become the greater me
or stay comfortable and let things be
I want to roar above the earth
to reach a new purpose and all it's worth
to say to myself I made it this far
to never look back and drive away in my car
my action depends on your directions
to walk in faith and feel no rejections
so I put my trust in you today
and pray you will find me a new way.

# Eyes TWO See

With two not one, but never the same
one stayed true, the other went insane
I prayed to God for my heart to let up
the pain, the lies, the betrayal, I never knew what was up
Why would you do me so wrong when I always did right?
I stood by like a stab of knife
that pierced your side, but never your back
to see with eyes so blinded by you
our bond was a lie and never was true

My truth was told, my secrets unfold
my words were twisted, my trust conflicted
to try to poison the ones I stood by
you took my words and said goodbye

You wanted royalty at the expensive of my loyalty
a spotlight you craved, that no man can see
I would have let you win if that was
all you wanted from me
I didn't care for the glitz and the fame
I stayed number two, I stayed in my lane

I could never fit in as number three
you had another side no one could ever see

The pain you left wounded deep
the tears, the flesh, the soul to keep

I cried many days, I cried many nights
the vision of us was just a sight
two wrongs made it right
to hold and to let go of something once tight

I free you to life, I free you to be
for my life goes on, my life is free
I am happier now than I ever thought I could be
thank you for unfolding my eyes so I can finally see.

# Losing My Identity

## Losing My Identity

In this life, it's important to stay in the light
trying to stay up and trying to do right
thoughts of seeing the world around
while keeping my head up and never staying down
life has handed me some good and some bad
holding on was the only chance I had
trying to keep up with never losing me
who I am is all I know how to be

I look in the mirror and say to myself
*"Hold, Sista! Hold on to life's wealth!"*
rising up in serenity while holding onto my identity
to the big butt, to huge titties and round hips

The vanity to insanity
the insecurity to impurity
from the secret society
the lies that hide in me
to wanting to be the figment on TV
the confusion of me and who I want to be

What hides inside is greater than the look that lies outside
be brave in who you are and never try to hide
because your true identity is what lies inside.

# Who I Am

## Who I Am

Who I am and Who I claim to be
the image of the Most High who created me
I am tall and fine but one of a kind
beautiful soul that is pure as gold

The life I seek was humble and meek
your love is strong, your love is never weak
the bond we share could never compare
to the love you give despite the life I lived
On my knees I say in prayer
help me get rid of these bad layers

I gave up the fight to receive your light
you gave me vision, you gave me sight
you took my heart and guided me
gave me a life I thought I'd never see

Visions of your blessings that came to be
you manifested them in honor of me
and in your arms is where I'll be

with the one who saved me.

# The Only One

## The Only One

The beginning of life, the beginning of sight if
the sky is blue, then I know his word is true
Why do we doubt the things we cannot see
but believe in the words spoken that deceives?
expression of a love with an empty heart
is like separating the cold from the winter apart

In the eyes of the one who sees
the world filled with so much disease
sickness of the mind, and souls left behind
the invasion of the spirits
praying to idol gods who don't hear it

How can you let your faith surrender?
when He speaks his voice roars like thunder
believe in the one whose love is unconditional
with a strong passion to save us intentionally
so believe in Him with all your heart
and in your life you will get a fresh start.

# Finally See

## Finally See

I take a look at my life and see so much blessings
I have finally let go and stop guessing
I stopped wondering if my life was ever complete
from a vision of my emptiness that left me waist deep
my love has grown through the branches of wheat

To find myself finally complete
to love, to die is who I am
I live to love and die complete
for who I am I can finally meet
to see myself and be pleased beyond what I'll ever seek

To feel betrayed and still rise from the ashes
my love I still give even if you trashed it
for me I gained something you lost
the love that warmed, to heal, to touch
though my heart hurts too much
I choose to let go, I choose to let it be such
but even though one will never be the same
I will remain strong in vain

Thank you for showing me who I can be
for one face is one and never two to see
for twins were separated as it was supposed to be
I stand alone, I stand with me
to see what I can be
in life without you and me.

# If I Could Just

If I could just save one life
then I know I have done something right
if I could just help someone cope
then I know that I have given them hope
if I could just stand strong
even when people try to knock me down
if I could just wipe every tear that falls from your face
and give you my shoulder with a warm embrace
if I could just tell you to be strong
and sometimes in life things just go wrong
if I could just grab your hand
and by your side I will stand
if I could just fight with you till the very end
my life, my love will help you mend.

# The Seed

## The Seed

Inspiration comes with great dedication
to stand in the light, with a soul so bright
the heart so pure, makes you feel secure
the blessings that fall, when you give him a call
the trust sustains the heart once in pain

A seed of light, blossom to great spiritual height
abundance of love given from the heart
one that covers all wounds right from the start
a man I love whom I have never seen
his presence is pure, his presence is clean

One that turned a heart once mean
mighty and brave I stand with you
given the kind of strength that split one in two
power and domain you gave to me
to stand in your presence, I stand set free

A seed of freedom, a seed of peace
it's a state of mind that can help you release

the passion inside, keeps the love inclined
to be in the light, you must live right

So, the planted seed is a seed of hope
use this journey to help someone cope.

# Set Me Free

How do I grow, when I have so much to show?
Where do I start seems to be the hardest part?
How do I leap when the edge is too steep?
How will I know when it is time to go?

A place I desire is far but near
How do I share these gifts that are so rare?
praying my talents will never fade
because of me being so afraid

Afraid to grow, afraid to be free
afraid to fail and afraid to lead
How do I have so much to give?

But afraid of a life I want to live
I desire a life where I am free
to grow into who I am called to be
to fight back the fear and start my career

So I rose up and started walking

but let God do all the talking

for His strength I remain
to a life that I will soon gain

My growth requires a big leap
and that is faith and belief
so with that I will say
get up and get out of your own way.

# The Passion to Create

A desire to create

the love, the fate

the passion that streams

the heart that beams

the lights so bright, the hold so tight

the warmth, the touch, to love just right

the words that soothe, the body the moves

the eye, the stare, the look so rare

the bite, the lips, the kiss on my hips

the heat, the fire, the soul, the flame

the way you scream my name

love so deep, the passion so sweet

the hearts that beats, the soul complete

the night is done, the morning begun

the moment I gave you our only son.

# Beauty in the Face of a Battle

How do you smile when the tears roll down your face?
How do you find peace with a heart
filled with so much rage?
How do I see the beauty in me with
the eye blinded from love?
How do I find beauty in it all?

Beauty is beyond the surface deep
Beauty is the soul that God keeps
Beauty is the awakening of a love never tried
Beauty is the love in his eye

Beauty is picking up the pieces of your life
Beauty is getting back up when life knocked you down
Beauty is the battle you win when all hope is lost
Beauty is the face you make searching for better days

Beauty is the hope you wear like a long red cape
Beauty is the step you take with a heart of faith
Beauty is He who walks with me

Beauty is not the face of the battle

Beauty is the journey you overcome.

# About The Author

Tameika Rahming is an avid poet and first-time published writer. Born in Toronto, Canada she migrated to the United States at the age of thirteen where her passion for writing became a way to release her inner pain and struggle to fit in. Through writing, she discovered peace and a divine connection to the spirit of God.

At the age of twenty-three, Tameika was diagnosed with aggressive Stage 1 Vulva Cancer. Through sickness, she found strength in the face of adversity and through her victory she found her faith and the will to fight.

Now nine years cancer-free, Tameika is married to her best friend and soulmate for ten happy years. She has two fur babies: a maltese named Snoopi and a yorkie named Bella.

www.ingramcontent.com/pod-product-compliance
Lightning Source LLC
Chambersburg PA
CBHW051736290426
43661CB00123B/631